# POETRY:
# HOW TO GET PUBLISHED
# HOW TO GET PAID

Writers' Bookshop

# POETRY:

## How to Get Published
## How to Get Paid

Kenneth C Steven

Published by Writers' Bookshop 1998
7-11 Kensington High Street,
London W8 5NP

Edited by Anne Sandys
Typesetting by Forward Press Ltd

# Contents

*For Ute, who helped me survive so many rejection slips.*
*With love.*

# Foreword

It's probably true to say that at no time before have so many people been writing poetry. There are poems on buses, poems on radio, poems in shop windows. But it's also probably true to say that never before have so many people been trying desperately to gain an audience for their poetry. More often than not, many of them end up miserable because they don't really know how to start.

This book shows you how you can beat the odds and see your work in print - and gain a financial reward into the bargain. It takes courage, much determination, a bit of luck, and a poet who's already producing good pieces of work. This book aims to encourage at every turn; to provide you with a variety of ideas so you can succeed in the poetry business, and achieve your ambitions despite all that the gloom merchants tell you.

First and foremost, though, you must believe in your own work. You must believe that your poetry is worth something, that you have things to say which matter, which are just that bit different to all the elegies and sonnets and haikus that have been written before. You must believe in your writing (while still being able to listen to genuinely constructive criticism), however hard that may prove at times.

This book will provide you, I hope, with a map and compass. It cannot give you all of the signposts nor tell you what to do at every junction, for each road will be different and difficult in its own way. What I do hope is that it may make the journey easier.

# 1 GETTING THERE FROM HERE ?

- Poetic fitness
- Writers' groups
- Mind your language
- Reading

William Golding's first novel was *The Lord of the Flies* - it won him the Nobel Prize. A screenplay can be dashed off by a novice and snapped up by Warner Brothers the following summer. It can happen. But many writers, even experienced ones, don't realise that a different methodology is required to get a first collection of poems published. So why should poetry be different to other genres?

Well, to begin with, there is very rarely a large pot of gold for a new poet. That isn't to say that there isn't money around for poets, but it is fair to say it's harder to come by and in less generous quantities. Those who do invariably profit from these winnings are the well-known poets, the 'names.' If you are at the top of the tree in poetry, or at least already up in the higher branches, publishing a collection will be much easier. A new collection by Hughes or Heaney will sell at least 30,000 copies. A new poet's work and reputation is likely to be absolutely unknown to a publisher. Because of this they will almost certainly reject a collection from that poet, no matter how good the work may be. So how on earth do you see those poems in print? The answer is you must set about building up a track record.

# Poetic fitness

You have to prove to a publisher that you have what it takes to be on their list of poets. You have to show your muscles and your medals. This means you have to have got yourself a good C.V. as a poet, i.e. your work published widely in journals and newspapers here in Britain and preferably overseas as well. It means you have to have plucked up the courage to undertake literary readings of your work, because poetry publishers are well aware of the fact that often many more poetry books sell at such events than in bookshops. In short you have to be good at marketing yourself in this cynical age when economic viability, not classical idealism, is what publishers want.

To begin with, you have to have a belief in your own poetry. I don't just mean that you are convinced it is great - that's not sufficient. When you have got a small collection of poems together let a select circle of people read and evaluate them. Don't choose 'yes-men;' there's no point being told your work is brilliant by friends and family who'd hate to disappoint you. Choose people who will give you an honest evaluation, who have some kind of an appreciation of literature or who are involved themselves in the writing/publishing world. If all of them say your work needs honing, the chances are it does. If the majority feel you are wonderful at poems that describe your inner state but not nearly so good at portraying rural landscape, then concentrate on that strong side. Often other people's insights will reveal to you truths you yourself would never have seen.

# Writers' groups

That's why a writers' group can be a boon. If there is one in your area, then consider going along at least for a time. This may well provide you with a chance to read your work to a small audience and to hear their reactions. You may also be lucky enough to meet like-minded people with whom you can share ideas and projects, and from whom you can gain encouragement.

But join a writers' group with caution. Some well-established clubs become like families; either they praise each other's work without ever daring to pass negative comment, or else they are only too eager to pour scorn on newcomers' work in a snobbish manner. I ran away from a writers' group when I was a tender teenager; it was dominated by a retired colonel who damned every piece of writing he didn't personally approve of. Writers' groups can seriously damage your health; tread carefully and if in doubt, leave. A writers' group can be a help, but it can also be a hindrance. I'm still not an active member of one and I don't feel I've suffered one bit!

# Mind your language

A word on language at the very outset. Obviously different poets have different styles, just like any other writers, but the language we use has to be looked at carefully.

In the first instance I'm talking about archaic language versus contemporary language. Quite often when I'm marking competitions I come across entries full of 'ere' and 'whither,' 'thou' and 'maiden.' It's not a good idea to do this, quite simply because we don't go around using Shakespeare's English unless we happen to be acting in one of his plays. Your language can be dignified and poetic, but it should not contain stereotypical words that are just not used in common speech or writing today. The only exception to this might be if you are writing a historical poem, recreating, let us say, the last words of Mary Queen of Scots before she faced her executioners. But even here you don't need to attempt to adopt old-fashioned language; just look at W.H. Auden's famous poem on the Roman soldier in Britain and you'll see what I mean.

The other important thing I want to mention concerns swearing and blasphemy. Contemporary literature has pushed back the boundaries of what is acceptable to the very limits, so that some infamous novels come across more as a flow of swearwords than much else. The problem is that if you use strong language to that extent it loses its impact on the reader and becomes redundant. My advice to you is to think very carefully before using strong language of any kind in your poetry. Ask yourself why you are using it. Is there a significance behind it or are you simply trying to be trendy? As long as you can justify your use of strong language convincingly there is not a real problem, but make sure you know where you stand on this before you run into criticism.

# Reading

It's probably true to say that at no time before have so many people been writing. Part of that's to do with the greater amount of free time that folk have, and also the interest that has sprung up in providing greater leisure services for the retired. More people, too, are aware of the potential rewards to be gained from writing blockbusters, bodice rippers and biographies.

In the poetry world things are no different. There are literally hundreds of small press poetry magazines and journals in Britain alone, and new ones spring up every week.

The problem is that people are, by and large, writing more than they are reading. I know I've often been guilty of this myself and still have to push myself to read my weekly quota of prose and poetry. But reading is vitally important. As writers we need to know what is being published and what succeeds. We also need to read the poetry and prose of yesteryear which has been adjudged to be great. We may be certain we want to write free verse, but understanding the magic of the sonnet and being able to produce rhyming couplets is no bad thing. I've often been told by art teachers that the best painters are always first-class drawers too. As a child you need to be able to walk before you can run.

So, as poets, we have to work at this reading business. We need to read the contemporary stuff as well as the classic stuff, even if we don't much care for it. New poetry books are often very expensive, so take advantage of your library service and order Wendy Cope's latest collection or the collected poems of John Masefield.

Try to subscribe to one or two poetry magazines to find out what their likes and dislikes are. If you can, visit the South Bank Centre in London or the Poetry Library in Edinburgh to browse through a whole range of past and present publications. Sometimes it may be very tempting to live in that ivory tower of poetry, but ultimately it won't do us any good. You have to be able to speak with authority about what your likes and dislikes are in contemporary poetry, you have to know the work of the top literary outlets so you can stand a chance of getting published there.

No matter how successful you may become, don't stop reading.

# 2 GETTING A NAME IN THE? JOURNALS

- The journals
- The covering letter
- The submission
- Anthologies
- Competitions
- Simultaneous submissions
- Waiting for a reply
- Keeping a record of your work

As I stressed in the opening chapter, building up a reputation in the literary magazines and journals is of fundamental importance to a poet starting out. But where do you begin? There are literally hundreds of magazines catering for poets in Great Britain, ranging from the big glossies like *Poetry Wales* or *Stand* to stapled together pamphlets produced in attics and garages. How do you know the great from the small before you start? Here *The Writer's Handbook* and the *Writers' and Artists' Yearbook* are frankly of very little assistance. They provide long lists of poetry outlets but have no space to outline the standard of each journal or its particular requirements. I have attempted to compile a directory of some of the most reliable journals in Britain and abroad at the back of this book, but if you want a comprehensive picture you will really need to subscribe to a whole range of magazines or visit the Poetry Library in London. Sometimes writers' groups will have a library of poetry books and journals as a resource for their members but this will be more a case of luck than anything else. I myself never saw any journals at all when I started out. I fired work blindly at everything from *Poetry Review* to *Planet*, working on the principle that if you throw sufficient mud some of it has to stick in the end. Once I had work accepted I was of course sent a copy of the journal, so bit by bit I built up a picture of the scene. It's one way of doing it, but I don't recommend the process.

# The journals

This diagram gives a rough outline of the hierarchy of the top British poetry outlets. It does not include newspapers which are in a sense a category of their own.

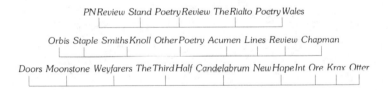

It may be that as an unknown poet you will be fortunate enough to get writing straight into *P.N. Review* or *Stand*. But quite frankly, like everywhere else, reputation helps. It is certainly said that trying to get work taken for outlets like the *London Review of Books* or the *T.L.S.* is pretty hopeless unless you are already known. So starting here is hardly advisable. I advise beginning with a mixture of the very small magazines - like those on the third row of the diagram - and one or two of the middle-ranking journals. At the beginning what you need more than anything else is confidence, and getting into any of these magazines will give you a rightful feeling of success. It will also provide you with a very important commodity - friends.

Once you have built up confidence with the smaller outlets and can face the slings and arrows of the big boys, try your luck with them. There are things to go on: *Poetry Wales* and *New Welsh Review* prefer Celtic-orientated and generally more rural writing. *Stand* is rather the opposite, having a fairly *Guardian*-like feeling to many of its poems and short stories. Social issues and struggle are at the heart of a great percentage of the creative output, and this is true of Scottish productions like *Chapman* and *West Coast Magazine* too.

It goes without saying that from now on you have to accept the day-to-day reality of rejection slips. All poets have to get used to them, and even the greats go on suffering them. One of my friends, who runs a small magazine near Glasgow, told me he rejected some of Seamus Heaney's poems just before the poet received his Nobel Prize. I could paper the house, let alone a room, with the rejection slips I've received.

Some hurt more than others. But you have to remember that there are several reasons for material being unacceptable, it's not automatically true that your work was just bad. It may have been bad timing; maybe an issue had newly been completed and the editor didn't want to stock-pile more material right away. Perhaps poems on a very similar theme to yours had just been accepted, maybe it was just a bad day... A standard rejection slip says little at all, but don't assume the worst about your work and throw your typewriter into the Thames. Bear in mind that a literary magazine like *Stand* may receive upwards of thirty thousand unsolicited poems a year. That's right, thirty thousand. That makes six hundred poems a week. Don't let odds like that make you give up, but bear in mind nonetheless that the competition is stiff and that many factors can come into play to decide whether or not your poems make it.

# The covering letter

Many poets seem to think this is an unnecessary addition to a submission of poems, almost a waste of time. Experience tells me that's quite wrong; a covering letter can do a great deal to aid the reception your poems get. A friendly introduction will do your chances no harm. Perhaps the six poems you are submitting were all inspired by a study tour to Eastern Europe, or by a visit to Gaelic-speaking communities in Ireland. Then mention that. It gives you, the poet, a human face, prepares the way for the editor's reading of your work.

Of course it's possible to damage your reception by enclosing an essay, not a letter. There is no need to antagonise a busy editor by going into great detail describing the latest weather in Skegness. You will find your own perfect covering letter in the end; the one I use to new magazines takes me all of half a minute to write now, it is so deeply engrained in my pen!

Your letters will change as you get to know individual editors who have used your work before. This is one of the spin-offs of working as a freelance writer; by and by you find real friends among the editors of magazines you write for. There are perhaps a dozen editors between Cornwall and Cape Wrath I would happily call on if I happened to be passing, such is the rapport we've built up over the years. Here, at any rate, is the kind of letter I used when I was starting out.

Dear Louise Taylor,

Please find enclosed six fairly recent poems which I'd ask you to consider for *Boom*. They were written while I was still working as a geologist for British Nuclear Fuels in Wales and concern many of my own thoughts on the industry at that time.

Several of my poems were recently used on local radio here in Liverpool and the feedback from listeners was very positive.

I look forward to hearing from you in due course.

Yours sincerely,

*Peter Roberts*

Peter Roberts

The first thing to note from the content of the letter is the use of the editor's name. Try to find this out, by hook or by crook, because it establishes a more personal contact and also looks as if you've done your homework on the magazine. Secondly, make mention of any kind of track record your poems have. Even if none has been published, then mention that a number of people have been encouraging your writing and urging you to get some of it published or whatever.

Later on, when your poetry has appeared in various journals around the country, mention perhaps three or four in a covering letter, but don't list all twenty-six. It's obviously counter-productive to appear arrogant to an editor you're trying to appeal to.

## The submission

Each submission should contain perhaps between five and eight poems. It can contain fewer but definitely not a greater number than that. Only one poem should appear on a single sheet of A4, and at all costs get access to a typewriter or a printer. Hand-written poems may still be considered and accepted by some small outlets, but you are prejudicing your own chances by submitting in this manner, and the sooner you invest in an Olivetti the better. I still thump out poems (and everything else) on an ancient typewriter, having an inbuilt distrust of computers. But my covering letters are all hand-written, and providing your writing is fairly legible then I suggest you do the same.

Don't forget to include a stamped addressed envelope with your submission. If you do not, the chances are Smith or Smedley will bin your poems with a snort of rage, not having got as far as reading them. But use second class stamps; the odds are you'll wait six or eight weeks for a reply anyway, so what's the point of wasting money on first class postage?

# Anthologies

Every year new poetry anthologies appear across Britain and indeed across the world. The first thing to point out is that a number of these are in fact run by vanity operators, i.e. people who aren't going to pay you for your poem but ask you to pay for the privilege of seeing it in print. Don't touch them with a barge pole, and tell everyone else not to into the bargain. You can sniff out vanity publishers of anthologies easily after a bit of practice; they promise, for example, to publish the work of two hundred poets in a volume entitled *Flowers of the Golden Children*, and this will be available to you at the 'specially reduced rate of £29.95, and available with a mahogany cover...'

But many worthy publishers produce high quality anthologies, often on countryside topics or featuring authors from a particular region or background. The anthologies of Poetry Now in Peterborough have proved particularly successful, and have helped many frustrated poets see their work in print for the first time. Keep your eyes peeled for genuine adverts requesting poets to submit their work. Cassell produce anthologies on various topics -

and a couple of years ago an American publisher took one of my poems for an anthology on herons! Every year New Writing Scotland produces an anthology of previously unpublished poetry and short stories from writers in Scotland. Some of the larger literary publishers do the same in England; it might focus on women's writing, on people's reactions to the war in Yugoslavia, on the death of Princess Diana, or whatever.

Find copies of anthologies like these in bookshops and take a note of them. Write to these publishers and ask if they are planning further such titles and if so, what type of poetry they are looking for. In the beginning, half the battle is knowing what is going on where; it is about keeping your ear to the ground and picking up on every available opportunity. Luck does play a part, but so does sheer, dogged Holmes and Watson sleuthing.

Anthologies matter because they look good mentioned in your C.V. and thus increase your standing, and because many of them pay fairly generously for the work they accept.

Writers' group anthologies can also be useful, but many are let down by poor production standards, bad editing and amateurish design quality. If you are going to do a thing, do it well. Make sure the editing is carried out strictly and meticulously, and make sure the finished product looks as good as it possibly could. What is the point of wasting tremendous writing with rotten production? But a good-looking, well-written anthology can do both a group's and an individual poet's reputation no harm at all.

Some outlets for anthology publication:

- *Poetry Now, Anchor Books and Triumph House*
  1-2 Wainman Road, Woodston, Peterborough, PE2 7BU
- *Poetry Today*
  Upper Dee Mill, Llangollen, LL20 8SD, Wales
- *New Writing Scotland*
  University of Glasgow, 9 University Gardens, Glasgow G12 8QH
- *Cassell plc*
  Wellington House, 125 Strand, London WC2R OBB

# Competitions

Another way of building up your literary C.V. to boost your chances of having a full collection accepted is by entering poetry competitions.

You will see these advertised everywhere from supermarkets to undergrounds, the reason being that poetry competitions make a considerable amount of money for the people who run them. The average entry fee for the major competitions today is £5 per poem, so if the organisers receive five thousand poems they should have plenty left over after awarding a few thousand to the winner and a few runners-up prizes.

Winners of the most prestigious contests often go on to become well-known as published poets: Don Paterson, Kathleen Jamie and Jo Shapcott are just three whose reputations were greatly enhanced by carrying off laurel wreaths in some of the majors.

Do beware, however, before pouring all your savings into the myriad of poetry competitions around the country. Have a look at the type of writing which is winning awards at the moment. Much of this trendy poetry is concerned with inner-city realism and the harshness of twentieth century life; poems about flocks of swans or golden daffodils are less likely to win prizes. Bearing this general point in mind, do consider each competition carefully on its merits.In time you will get a sense of the literary likes and dislikes of individual judges, and can decide whether or not it's worth forking out a fiver for an entry.

I personally prefer the smaller, more local, contests to the giants. The odds of winning a prize are higher because the organisers, with less money to spend on advertising, will have received fewer entries. The big boys (and girls) of the poetry world are also less likely to bother entering. In addition, entry fees tend to be more reasonable; you might pay one or two pounds per poem but not more. In such competitions you might find a first prize of perhaps five or six hundred pounds; not to be sneezed at by any writer struggling to make ends meet!

Writing competitions in general are a bit like gambling. You're sure the piece you're entering is going to win and you're willing to put your money where your mouth is. Most of the time you get it wrong; but once every so often if you're lucky your hunch proves to be right.

But luck is the operative word. Judging competitions is a highly subjective business. I know because I'm often asked to do it myself, and struggle to keep as open a mind as possible. But I'm fully aware that like any other judge I'm drawn to the type of work I like best and for which I will have an inbuilt preference.

So enter competitions in strict moderation, and now and again use that tenner, instead, to buy a second-hand copy of Wallace Stevens' poetry or a ticket to a reading by Seamus Heaney. I know which option will do your poetry more good....

(A list of some of the poetry competitions to watch out for will be found at the end of the book.)

## Simultaneous submissions

Many poets beginning to send their writing out for the first time rightly wonder if they should send the same poems to two or more outlets at the one time.

My own attitude is that magazines have no reason to expect that poets will dutifully wait until they have a response from the first outlet before sending the same work to the second. A poet's lot is not an easy one. If Smedley from *Colussus* sits on your very best material for half a year and more, why should you not have the right to allow Simons from *Taurus* to see the same poems and make a decision in two months? If magazines want to be treated with the respect they feel they are due, then they have to begin by treating their writers fairly. I appreciate that many editors receive groaning postbags day in, day out, but that gives them no excuse to lose material or to return it many months later with coffee stains and crossings-out.

So do send your new, great poem to several outlets at the one time. But remember to keep a careful record of where each poem has travelled and don't get caught out. The danger is if two big magazines (who will know each other's publications well) both accept the same poem. You will be extremely unpopular if the piece appears in both, and you even risk being blacklisted. You will certainly face problems ever getting these two outlets to accept your poetry again.

If for some reason this does happen, don't do nothing. You must decide which of the two is going to be of more benefit to you in the long run. Then you will have to write to the other and apologise profusely for your error and withdraw your poem there and then. With any luck you will be forgiven and the editor will bear no grudge against you. However, if your poem is accepted for *Poetry Review* and for the *Diddlebury Women's Institute Quarterly*, I wouldn't worry unduly. The chances are that the editor of *Poetry Review* is not an avid reader of the *Diddlebury Women's Institute Quarterly*.

# Waiting for a reply

How long do you sit impatiently waiting for that editor's reply? The answer is really in your own hands, but it is not a good idea to start phoning up a fortnight after submitting poems to find out what the reaction was. Editors may not always be as busy as they claim to be, but busy they certainly are, and attempting to cajole them into a decision will only have one result. Believe me, I've been there. Never phone a poetry editor, that's my advice. Not unless you know this individual very well and have found him or her to be in constant good spirits. Phone, perhaps, to ask about when your work is to appear or about the cheque which should have arrived and hasn't, but don't ring up to demand news of your last submission. It doesn't look good. If weeks and months have rolled by since you submitted work and you can justify asking for news, then drop the editor a postcard. But make it as friendly as possible and keep the tone light. Playing with a lion's tail is always dangerous. The best cure for impatience is to send out new work somewhere else. Keep the pot boiling; then you will not be waiting for one vital reply and a possible big disappointment.

## Keeping a record of your work

If you intend to take up this battle seriously, then you need to be organised about it. Be a Byron by night, but do your homework by day. It will pay dividends.

In a notebook make a list of the outlets you have sent poetry to. When I do this, I mention after each magazine title the individual poems it has received; in this way there isn't a danger of sending any outlet the same work over again. It also means I can have an overview of what poems are 'on the market' and which 'on the shelf.' At any one time I will have anywhere between 100 and 150 poems being considered by journals, but even if you have only ten or a dozen pieces doing the rounds, you need to ensure you have a note of where they are. Beside each submission listing I leave a space so that I can either place a tick there if one or more poems is accepted, or more usually a cross when I have been unsuccessful. I list my submissions month by month so that I can also look back to see how long ago it was since I inflicted work on *The Scrooge* or had yet another crack at getting into *Missing Link*. I also dutifully note my income because eventually poetry earnings can come to interest the taxman.

I also strongly urge you to keep another notebook where you can store the names of useful contacts, magazines and publishers you discover by chance, the addresses of competitions, etc. If you're serious about this you will over time become a detective, your poetry spectacles rarely far away. If you go to readings or are leafing through magazines and flyers at the local bookshop, then have this notebook to hand so you can make a note of any new information that might help your cause. Once you are conducting your own readings, you also need to be on the look out for adverts for writers' groups and literary gatherings, where a poet might prove to be a very welcome guest.

All this may seem fussy and not very important, but as they say, it takes many droplets to make the ocean.

# 3 READINGS

- Starting out
- Preparation
- Looking good
- Going solo
- The content
- Finance

I think many aspiring poets look on these much as most mortals look on dental appointments. I know I did to begin with, and I still find visits to secondary schools rather like having to cross crocodile-infested water. But there's no way round this if you want to stand a serious chance of having a collection taken on by a publisher. I reiterate that most poetry books sell through readings, not through bookshops, and publishers are as aware of that fact as poets.

But you don't need to book the Albert Hall for your first venue. Small is beautiful, and small in this case is also less intimidating. You must at all costs aim to build your confidence, not to destroy it altogether.

A few years back when I finally accepted the awful truth about having to do readings, I undertook one in the town of Paisley outside Glasgow. Quite blithely I took along all my poems of country and coast, never considering what type of material would be presented by the other invited poets. The man before me read a delightful prose poem about the murder of an old man and his little dog, and the poems that had come before were all concerned with gang violence, drugs and general cruelty. I felt like getting up when it was my turn and saying, 'Look, I shouldn't be here at all. I'll come back some other time. Bye.' But was too late for that . My poems went down like lead weights in a duck pond. I crawled off the stage in tatters and it was a long time before I had the confidence to read again.

# Starting out

To begin with then, make very sure that you're comfortable with the people you're reading with and the kind of environment you have as a venue. Later on once you have built up your confidence and know that you can present your poetry and present it well, this will be far less of a consideration. I have enough wisdom to steer clear of some very specific inner city events, but I rarely turn down an opportunity to read.

I suggest that you do a reading first with either one person or with a group of folk whose work you know and who have given encouragement to your own poetry in the past. They may be members of your writers' group, they might be contributors to one of the magazines in which your work has also appeared, or whatever.

I suggest this because undertaking the whole programme alone to start with is a tall order. Apart from anything else it requires reading a great number of poems! If you read as part of a larger circle, you yourself are likely to be able to choose how many pieces you will present. Even having the opportunity to read two or three short poems will give you a first important injection of confidence.

# Preparation

I've been at many readings where poets got up on the stage and began, 'I've...er...got a couple of ...well... poems I wrote quite a long time ago, actually. They are...er...you know, things I felt quite strongly about, actually.' I'm not just writing this to be nasty, I'm writing it because I felt extremely sorry for the poets concerned. This is not how to get the public on your side, nor how to create an impression. This is not how to sell yourself, or to sell books.

Now I am no born orator, believe me. I am softly spoken, and after long and horrible years at school, I don't have a vast amount of confidence. It's obvious that the poets who began their reading like that had very little confidence too, but then that's all the more reason to go prepared!

I never undertake a reading without having gone through in my head what I'm going to present. I write down the gist of my programme so that I know the order of things and can work out roughly how long I will speak for. (If you're told to read for an hour and you dry up after ten minutes you're in trouble, and vice versa.) If you can, find a quiet place at home where you can rehearse your programme. Try to memorise the gist of it so you don't have to read from the paper but rather use what you've written as notes. If you can, think of a couple of funny comments to begin your programme; it will give you confidence and it will make the audience warm at once to you and what you have to say. Make an ironic comment about your nervous state, about the fact that this may be your first and last reading, etc. It's good policy to build up a little stock of stories which you can use to warm up audiences. I'm not suggesting you have to become a stand-up comedian, but melting the ice is always of value, and such an approach will always help you through those first five dreadful minutes, in particular.

# Looking good

I suppose this is a subjective point, but I reckon it's worth looking your best at a poetry reading. Some poets turn up in torn jeans and a rather sheepy pullover, looking as though they had just popped over from the protest to the new terminal at Manchester Airport.

Now don't get me wrong, most of my friends fall into the sheepy category, indeed I would consider myself pretty sheepy. But if you want to be taken seriously as a writer, then you have to look serious about it. I know that Wendy Cope makes a point of wearing a suit at her readings because she considers poetry to be her professional career, and as a result she wants to be businesslike in the way she approaches it. I think it's important, too, because a large sector of society thinks poets, like all artists, get up for lunch, shave at Christmas and smoke roll-ups. The stereotype is amusing, but the treatment some people give artists is not. It's worth working to try to change that perception in society.

I'm not suggesting that everyone contemplating undertaking readings should go out and buy a complete new wardrobe at vast expense. Nor am I suggesting that you have to look as 'businesslike' as Wendy Cope. If someone put a tie round my neck before a reading I'd think I was back at school and go to pieces. At all costs, feel comfortable with what you choose to wear. Feel attractive, because this in turn will give you confidence when it is your turn to stand up to read.

# Going solo

When you begin to climb that poetry ladder and you are at last invited to do solo readings, organise things beforehand as much as you can.

If you feel more confident with a lectern then arrange to have one at the venue. (I recommend that you stand to read; older people in particular will grumble about not hearing sufficiently well, and your voice will carry better if you are on your feet.) Have a glass of water near at hand, not vodka. After half an hour in an airless hall your throat will feel like the runway at Heathrow, and as a poet you have to look after that throat of yours. But avoid alcohol before you begin; it's dangerous to start relying on a quick whisky 'to calm the nerves' every time. Reward yourself afterwards, not before.

If you are the sole reader, I suggest you speak for about three-quarters of an hour. If the audience is a school one, cut that to half an hour. There's no point reading to an inattentive audience or one that is starting to think about the tea and buns. I once read at a large conference on publishing poetry abroad, and after an hour I noticed that several elderly ladies had fallen asleep. It did not do my confidence much good.

If you have books out by this time, or information about your readings, make sure this is clearly displayed at the venue. After people have asked questions - if you want them to ask questions - inform them of the availability of publicity materials, books or whatever. It's worth having a clipboard and pen on your display table so that those interested in your work can be put on a mailing list. This means that when a book comes out, or a reading takes place in a certain area, you can target the individuals most likely to be interested.

Finally, after all readings, keep your ear to the ground. Don't vanish out of the hall like a scalded cat, stay to talk to people. It may be that you meet some eccentrics who want to know what your opinion is of Shelley's *Queen Mab* or the last part of some remote sonnet of Shakespeare's. But it may also be that Lady Denisa of Marlberry House wonders if you would be able to give a reading for her house party on Christmas Eve. Often you will meet important people at readings; important in the sense that they can offer new leads, assistance to get on. And struggling poets have to grab every chance they can.

# The content

Obviously, over time you will work out yourself the most successful format for your own readings. You will hear other poets presenting their work and learn what is successful in their programmes - as well as what is utterly dreadful! (I have listened to several extremely respected poets in the last years and in the main their presentations left an awful lot to be desired. I'm not sure whether that is comforting for us or worrying!) Read poems slowly, don't go through them as if you have a train to catch. Poetry is 'deep language;' an audience needs time to absorb metaphor and imagery, to grasp meaning. If you can, give even a brief introduction to individual poems. It always annoyed me when pop groups I loved just ploughed on with their programmes, giving no background information about what inspired one particular song or another. I knew something important must have been behind classic lyrics and melodies, and I wanted to have at least an inkling of the secret. Dare to share a little of yourself with an audience - they will want to know all the more.

## Finance

Obviously there are costs involved in organising and running any event, and a reading is no exception. Normally there is the hire of the hall to be considered, the expenditure on refreshments, publicity costs and your own expenses. There is little point running an event which is going to prove a significant drain on your own resources.

Whether acting alone or as part of a group, try at all costs to obtain financial support for the event. In the first instance, contact the Arts Council to see if they can help; it may be that the regional section will prove the most likely sponsors. The best bet is to do your homework as far in advance as possible; the Arts Council will send you detailed forms with questions concerning the event, and you will need to be clued up about your whole programme.

If you can include the reading in an Arts Festival then so much the better as it is likely they will carry the costs for your event, in addition to paying fees to the poets. You also stand a much better chance of getting a good audience, since the event will be listed in the Festival programme.

If neither of these options proves possible then approach your Council for advice. Because of the severe cuts in public spending of recent years, most councils are reluctant to finance so much as a tiddlywinks competition. All the same they will have a local arts programme, and exist to provide advice and assistance to individuals and groups in the district. They may at least provide a venue and some advertising for your event.

# 4 FOREIGN BODIES: PUBLISHING ABROAD ?

- Submitting poems
- General points
- The future
- Copyright

Getting published abroad as a poet is not by any means a prerequisite. There are so many top quality British Literary outlets that you could quite happily spend a lifetime getting into those, without ever troubling to conquer the North American and Antipodean ones.

But there are several worthwhile reasons for trying all the same. The first has, once again, to do with gaining a reputation. Word of publication in a Canadian or Irish literary outlet will do your C.V. no harm at all, and will show an editor that you are willing to go far (literally) to win credits. The second reason is a financial one. Although sending poetry abroad can be an expensive business, it can also win you considerable rewards. Payment rates for journals supported by the Australia Council, for example, are generous, and the competition is definitely not as tough as in Britain.

It becomes a bit of an addiction, I suppose. Having got a poem into one particular journal, a copy of the publication duly arrives. In it you discover advertisements for three more outlets in the same country. Now you'll hardly be able to wait to try poems on these newly-discovered journals. The bug has got you...

Remember to keep a balance, all the same. Submitting work abroad is time-consuming and often frustrating. Information about outlets may be out-of-date and unreliable: editors' editorial addresses may have changed, the journal will perhaps have folded. Checking information on British outlets can be difficult enough, but making sure all the details concerning a journal in Queensland are correct is another matter altogether.

Don't put all your eggs in one basket. Build up a steady knowledge of one or several journals abroad, and be faithful to these. Don't scatter poetry about the globe in a desperate bid to become famous overnight, because you will only be left frustrated and very out of pocket.

# Submitting poems

Most of us, especially impecunious poets, are pretty traditional when it comes to technology, and I am assuming that the majority of people submitting work abroad will do so by conventional postal mail.

I have already mentioned more than once the potential expense of sending poetry to foreign journals. For that reason you have to think of all ways possible to keep the cost of submissions to the minimum.

Now I am lucky in that most of my poems are short, on average between twelve and fifteen lines in length. I know that you are constantly reminded to submit each poem on a separate sheet of paper, but when dealing with foreign outlets this would prove quite impossible. My solution is to put four or five separate poems onto two sides of an A4 sheet, thus saving a lot of paper and a lot of weight!

Often I choose poems which have been successful in Britain and which people have liked particularly. So I will submit poems published previously in this country, though whether that is strictly 'cricket' or not I don't know. I haven't been extradited yet.

Just because I want to keep the weight of the submission down, though, doesn't mean I miss out on a covering letter. This is just as important as with a submission to a British outlet, indeed it is perhaps even more vital. There is all the more need for a foreign editor to know 'where you are coming from.' But don't use a full sheet of A4 if you can help it; instead get hold of one of these small pads with postcard sized sheets.

This might be a letter to a new outlet in Australia:

Dear Mr. Hackett,

I heard of your journal recently, and I am submitting several poems for consideration. I apologise that all the work appears on one single sheet of A4, but this is the most effective way of submitting when postage is so ridiculously expensive.

My poetry has appeared in a number of British journals and in *Back Beat* in Canberra. Many of my poems concern my years spent in the army and detail experiences in Northern Ireland and the Falkland Islands.

Yours sincerely

*Peter Roberts*

Peter Roberts

# General points

At the end of the book I have included a checklist of some of the outlets I have found success with. Obviously this is by no means exhaustive: if you are really keen to pursue this publishing line, then a book I have found extremely helpful is the *Poet's Market*. This is an American hardback book big enough to kill a horse. It contains listings of poetry outlets world-wide, but concentrates naturally enough on the North American journals. What is useful about this handbook is that it provides the reader with background information on each magazine: the standard of work accepted, the approximate time taken to deal with submissions, the type of writing particularly sought after, etc. Recently I discovered the Writers' Bookshop's own series of handbooks on poetry outlets in the U.S., Australia, and Britain itself. Again, valuable information is supplied regarding each separate listing.

But a word of caution. The various outlets differ considerably from each other, and it is important to be aware of these differences. Try to evaluate which outlets seem most suitable for your poems, and which seem less appropriate in terms of style and level, particularly if you are starting out. Submitting poetry abroad is a much greater investment - often in terms of time as well as finance - so it is well worth stacking the odds as much in your favour as possible before you begin.

Every submission you put into the pillar box must contain at least one International Reply Coupon, because obviously you can't send a stamped addressed envelope to Hawaii or Hong Kong. The problem is that some areas are better than others at accepting IRC's. The Australians never seem to have any difficulty with them, whereas the Americans appear to dislike them intensely.

I have lost a vast amount of poetry, short stories and articles in America, and my publication record in the States is nothing short of diabolical. To begin with, I think the postal service in the States leaves a lot to be desired.

That is not just my own prejudice; a number of American friends have told me as much themselves. But I also believe the whole IRC system is not very well understood in America, so that some outlets may just destroy submissions rather than attempt to return them.

I am writing all this not to have a go at the Americans, but to warn you before you gleefully begin firing off poems to everywhere between Portland and Pennsylvania. The American market is temptingly huge, and temptingly lucrative, but look before you leap.

By contrast, the Canadian journals are most efficient at responding to submissions, and often very speedy. The top outlets, as in Australia, tend to be found within the country's universities, but in neither case does that mean that all the work accepted is frightfully intellectual or academic.

It was a surprise to find that whereas the Australian poetry scene is alive and thriving, the New Zealand situation is quite the opposite. Indeed the small clutch of journals I have discovered in New Zealand seem only willing to consider the work of their own writers and artists, or else that of New Zealanders abroad. One can only hope the situation may improve over the next few years.

A final point concerns money. Although you are unlikely to get rich quick from the profits of poems published abroad, you may well receive the odd helpful cheque in due time. However, bear in mind that most of these will be paid in dollars not pounds. Some of the truly large journals have the wherewithal to send sterling, but don't hold your breath. Because banks charge unbelievable amounts to cash foreign cheques (mine asks for over five pounds a time!) it is worth hanging on to cheques to cash two or more at one time. If you have a reasonably helpful bank they may well be persuaded to make just one charge for all the cheques. Don't see your hard-earned rewards robbed by the bank!

## The future

Our communications world is changing very fast. Already we can send electronic messages to Timbuktu at the press of a button. Frightening or fantastic, depending on your outlook, but one thing is certain: we are all going to have to get used to many of the changes that lie ahead. Even poets.

I think it may well be easier to send poems down a phone line than in an envelope. But quite where that leaves International Reply Coupons, copyright and the like I don't know. All I do know is that quite as many people ignore faxes as ignore letters, and I am not one of those who believes blue-eyed in the salvation of technology. If you already have access to the Internet or e-mail then search out the poetry corners across the world and see how successful submitting work in this way can be. Of course it has to be remembered that the vast majority of journals world-wide haven't moved at anything like the speed of oil companies and travel agencies and don't even have sites to access by computer.

One word of caution, however, concerning the domestic poetry scene. Be very wary of those offering to publish your work on the Internet at great expense; I think the benefits are pretty dubious to say the least. The Internet is very much flavour of the month, and these 'publishers' are jumping onto the bandwagon. Though the prospect may sound exciting, it is doubtful it will reap any great rewards at the moment.

# Copyright

Some poets starting out are paranoid the magazine or publisher to whom they submit their work will steal their poems. It's an understandable anxiety, but there's no need to be too anxious.

If anything is in genuine danger in the writing world it is Ideas. If you have a particularly brilliant brainwave about making a documentary on starfish off Newfoundland or the inventor of the bicycle pump, and submit these ideas to a television company, then you might be concerned about that. Cases have been brought - and successfully - against companies who declined someone's work and then went off with the idea to develop it themselves.

I have never yet heard of a magazine or publisher stealing a poem. Why should they? If it is good enough, they are likely to be all too quick to tell you; if it is not, they will reject the poem. The only place I can imagine it being possible to steal a poem is via the Internet, where someone reads a particularly good piece on the screen, copies it, and submits it to a journal as their own. But even that seems a pretty remote possibility.

If you are unconvinced by this and still want the security of formal copyright, then the easiest way to proceed is to post yourself the poem or poems concerned. The sealed envelope containing your work has been franked and can be produced as evidence in the event of someone pilfering your poems. The other even simpler solution is to write © and your name at the bottom of the last page of your typescript. No-one will dare risk stealing your work if you are claiming it has been formally copyrighted.

Unless otherwise stated, a magazine or publisher reproducing your poetry does not buy the copyright to the work. That remains with you, the author.

# 5 PREPARING A COLLECTION ?

- A good home
- Making advances
- Acceptance and rejection
- Down to business
- The alternatives
- The National Poetry Foundation
- Self-publishing
- Vanity publishing
- Small presses

Once you feel your poems have won their spurs and you can respond to all the possible demands publishers might make, then prepare for battle. It's difficult to say how many poems should make up a collection, because every publisher has different formats; thus a collection is really as long as a piece of string. This is not something to fret over, because any publisher seriously interested in taking on your work will tailor the collection according to their requirements.

It also depends to a certain extent on how you have put your collection together. The poems will probably either be all your best-known ones to date, the ones which have made most of a splash in the magazines and which have proved most popular with audiences, or else all those on one particular theme: poems concerned with the sea, with Africa, with the loss of a loved one, or whatever. With the second type it is important that all the poems are of a fairly similar standard. It is tempting to put in extra pieces which mean a great deal to you - but that isn't necessarily enough to satisfy a critical editor. Don't put in anything which might bring down the overall quality of the collection.

I think it's no bad idea at this stage to make three or four copies of the work to give out to individuals whose opinions you trust and who will give you honest, not kind, reactions. Ask them to mark any poems they find particularly weak, and see if these doubts are shared independently by the others. Sometimes it's very hard indeed to look objectively at your own work, particularly if the poems concerned have become very familiar to you. Don't ignore criticism, or worse, react badly to it. Take constructive criticism on board and look at your collection again in the light of it. Prune, if that is necessary, painful as it may be.

# A good home

There are obviously differences between the major publishers of poetry, but a truly strong collection should be admired wherever it lands. Poets dream of Faber, but to be given a home there requires a top class reputation in literary circles and, I suspect, a small quantity of good fortune. Tastes, I feel, have changed since the days when Hughes and Heaney started out there; Faber's new poets write very differently to the old vanguard. I'm not sure that poems about foxes or gathering brambles would prove so acceptable now...

Bloodaxe is not as fearsome as its name suggests, though much of the poetry pulls no punches. I feel often there is a strong social consciousness evident in the Bloodaxe poets; the great Welshman R.S. Thomas had his later work published here, as did the Russian Irina Ratushinskaya, whose protest poems from prison at the end of the cold war won her a huge audience. Jonathan Cape like controversial voices, and usually Scottish ones at that, but otherwise the larger publishers' tastes seem fairly eclectic, and you will just have to begin at the top and work your way down.

I don't believe in being unduly polite to publishers; they are very seldom polite to poets. It may seem honourable to let one copy of your collection go the rounds until it finds a home, but you may also see precious years of your life drift by while you wait. Several of my poetry collections which were submitted to top publishers are now missing presumed dead, others lingered there for innumerable months until my patience gave out and I requested them to be returned. Even if they do come back of their own accord, typescripts are often dog-eared, their covers have coffee stains and their pages smudges of black ink. Publishers have feet of clay, and very wobbly clay at that.

# Making advances

While not wanting to bend over backwards to please publishers, I do think it is worthwhile doing everything possible to safeguard a precious collection of poetry. For this reason, if you are daring to approach one or several of the large publishers, send on a letter first (enclosing an s.a.e.) so that your work will not arrive totally unsolicited and you will ascertain the name of the poetry editor who will receive your work. This latter point is of particular relevance. Large publishers with many divisions are rather like elephants: tusks, trunk, ears, tail, etc. It may take a long time for your typescript to get from ears to tail if you didn't get it there to begin with.

You don't need a long covering letter in the first instance, though a brief statement of your achievements to date will do no harm. If your handwriting is sufficiently legible then don't go to all the trouble of typing a letter. The same short piece can be used for several publishers, but do not photocopy your letter, whether it is typewritten or otherwise. Editors were not born yesterday, and this sort of mass production will win you no favours.

## The send off

When you get the all-clear from one or several publishing houses, complete your final preparations to the typescript and look forward to a long wait.

Whatever type of collection yours is, arrange the poems in the kind of order you would like to see in a finished book, and number the pages in pencil at the top right-hand corner. Don't go to enormous trouble over a cover, especially if you are also an artist, because the chances are this page will come back dismembered, and a lot of your precious labour wasted. This goes for illustrations in general: never submit them at the beginning of the whole battle. Publishers like to do things their way, and they do not take kindly to being told by any author how they want their book to look. 'My sister Jenny's a great artist,' is also the kind of talk which turns editors dark purple with rage. You can mention the idea of illustrating your collection if it seems particularly relevant (i.e. if you yourself are a professional artist) but do not push the point or you will antagonise the editor at once.

I generally include a sheet after the title page giving a brief run-down on the poems in the collection: what magazines or anthologies they have appeared in at home or abroad, mention of pieces broadcast on radio, etc. This is worthwhile; it is all about establishing the credentials of your work, and the more you can mention to boost its track record the better.

The covering letter you now write is of real importance. Obviously each one will be different, but the example overleaf provides an outline of the possible content.

## Acceptance and rejection

You would be extremely fortunate if your collection were to be accepted first time round. How wonderful if that were the norm, but it just isn't, often not even with authors who go on to become exceptionally well-known.

A few years ago I met an American lady who was a famous children's author. She was fairly elderly, and during her life she had seen a staggering number of her books published. But what was still fresh in her mind was

Dear Hilary Westbrook,

Thank you for your recent letter concerning my poetry collection - I have pleasure in sending this on to you now. There are forty-five poems in the *Killing Time* collection; all of these were inspired by the Gulf War and by the experiences of my own best friend, who was severely injured in the conflict.

Almost all the poems have been published, either here or in America. The best-known piece, *Dead and Buried*, was actually used in a recent television documentary on Gulf War Syndrome. This poem, and several others in the collection, were also broadcast on radio some months ago.

I have undertaken a great number of readings across the country in the last months, and have found that audiences are both challenged and moved by the poems from *Killing Time* in particular. This does not apply solely to library audiences; I have also been asked to visit several schools in the region to read from the collection and to discuss issues raised by the poems with senior school groups.

I have no doubt that this collection would succeed. A great number of people have inquired about obtaining copies already, and one or two head teachers have expressed interest in using the collection as a class text.

At any rate, I hope you will react positively to the poems here, and I look forward to hearing from you in due course.

Yours sincerely,

*Peter Roberts*

Peter Roberts

the fight she had had to get the first one into print. That children's book was rejected by eighty-three publishers before one said yes.

I hope it won't be that hard for you; I was certainly more fortunate. But I quote this example to show what tenacity you have to have if you really want to succeed, if you really believe your work deserves an audience. I have a rule with myself that whatever comes in rejected at breakfast-time is in the mail again by lunch-time. I do that because it keeps me buoyant, it means I am back in the fight and I have new hope of success. Sometimes doing that is far from easy and requires a tremendous amount of willpower. You will discover your own way to cope and to bounce back, but find it you must if you are serious about winning a place in the writing world.

## Down to business

If you do get that letter of acceptance, enjoy the moment to the full. It is a magnificent feeling to get a book accepted for publication; a bit like being told your baby is going to be born!

But don't just wait in a sea of bliss until the finished product arrives. There's hard work ahead of you, and your input will help to ensure the best results. Publishers have a nasty habit of disappearing at this stage, of doing everything themselves so that the author has as little chance of sticking their oar in as possible.

Recently I went to Edinburgh to meet the publishers of my latest poetry collection. I remember my shock when the editor took me over to the computer to show me the planned illustrations for the book. 'Do you think these will be all right?' she asked anxiously. Never before had I had dealings with an editor who cared what my opinion on the process was, let alone asked for it!

But first things first. Ask to have a contract sent to you as soon as possible. This document concerns the royalties you will receive on book sales, the number of free copies you will be entitled to, the terms of payment, and so on. More and more publishers try to get away with giving first-time authors lousy contracts, so don't just sign on the dotted line without a moment's hesitation. It is worth doing a bit of homework to make sure you are not being sold down the Swanee River!

A literary agent will evaluate a contract for you, but also take away at least 10% of your royalties for doing so. 10% may not amount to very much at the end of the day when it is from a poetry collection, but it is still 10% of your blood, sweat and tears!

If you are about to become a published author, the chances are that the Society of Authors will accept you as a candidate for membership. The Society exists first and foremost to provide moral support for writers; it also offers legal advice and has established a pension scheme for members. The Society will evaluate any publishing contract free of charge for one of its members, a very valuable service indeed.

# The alternatives

If you are told no by publishers again and again and again, what do you do? Other independent people respond to your poetry and it has been accepted in plenty of outlets, but no house will take you on. Perhaps your poetry is not viewed as being 'commercially viable' enough in an age when saleability counts for everything. The answer is not to throw your pen away and abandon all hope; here are the alternatives which are open to you - give them careful thought.

# The National Poetry Foundation

In 1993 I was in the depths of despair about my own poetry. I had had work published in many well-known journals both in Britain and overseas, and I knew I wasn't kidding myself that plenty of folk appreciated what I was writing. But my poetry was rural-based, and idealistic and rich in imagery. The big publishers wanted different material, and were busy publishing it. In despair I turned to the National Poetry Foundation, and through this organisation came to see my first collection published.

Membership of the NPF costs somewhere in the region of £20 per year. After this fee has been paid, members can submit batches of poems to Johnathon Clifford, co-founder of the Foundation, for his evaluation. A maximum of five poems can be contained in each batch, and poems are either accepted or rejected in the same way in which a journal would operate. Once forty poems or so have been deemed to be of sufficient merit for publication, the Foundation will bring out these pieces in a book at no further expense to the poet. This scheme is made possible by the very generous donations of funds to the Foundation by one lady in particular, Rosemary Arthur.

These books will not sell in great quantities. The Foundation do not possess the resources or the manpower to distribute its titles widely, so the onus is on the poets themselves to market their collections as effectively as possible. This means that poets must be prepared to start reading their work if they have not done so before. Not that the Foundation will put pressure on their poets to produce sales figures at the end of the year, not at all. But it is only sensible to do all you can to see your collection going out to people if you have fought long and hard for publication!

Johnathon is also very generous about the number of copies of any new collection that he sends out for review. The books themselves are A5 in size with fully laminated illustrated covers. Johnathon discusses at length both front cover illustrations and the content of back cover blurb with poets, and overall I was most satisfied with the look of our first published collection *Remembering Peter*.

The important thing about a Foundation publication is that it provides an up-and-coming poet with a first real stepping stone towards recognition. It will not bring fame, but it will bring fresh hope. It will bring reviews, a bigger audience, and the prospect of a mainstream publisher saying yes next time that bit more likely.

The one thing to bear in mind is that it can take many months and even years to build up a sufficient stock of poems with the National Poetry Foundation to allow for the publication of a first book. All editors are subjective in their tastes and Johnathon Clifford is no exception.

# Self-publishing

This is an option that more and more writers are choosing as production costs decrease all the time and technological wizardry increases all the time. But tread warily, there are landmines embedded in this particular bit of ground, and it's not worth getting injured...

I myself have never self-published anything, but my father has, so I have had the benefit of some fly-on-the-wall observation. The most significant advantage for writers who decide to opt for self-publishing is that after costs have been met the profits are all their own. The author who chooses to be conventional and to find a publisher in the usual way will be grateful to receive 10% of the sale price of the book once it is in the shops; in my case that amounts to 50p a copy most of the time. The author who chooses to self-publish his or her work may have a return of £3 per copy on a book which retails at a fiver. If this statistic proves anything, then it is that mainstream publishers are mean, but then you should know that by now anyway...

But here is the thing to remember, as well as losing the publisher you are also losing the benefits of the publisher. The self-publishing author's two greatest enemies are marketing and distribution, and both are hard nuts to crack unless you are prepared to invest a great deal of time and energy.

You need to work out all your target outlets beforehand, undertake as much homework as you can, to ensure that at the very worst you can recover your expenditure. And in working out your expenditure you must be certain you are not skimping on vital elements like cover design and quality, which are so important when it comes to 'hooking' a potential buyer. It is also imperative that the finished book is attractive enough to attract the likes of Waterstones and Dillons, who will be naturally wary of a self-published title.

Once again, readings will play an enormous part in ensuring that a self-published collection succeeds. In many ways, a local book that describes the waterfall above the town and the standing stones over the hill will do much better than a rather remote collection of poems about Tibet and the monasteries of Nepal. In the latter example you are offering something for a literary audience only, and immediately you will find the book appealing to 10% or less of the book-buying public. If you self-publish an attractive little volume of poems which has a familiar local name as a title, and which contains many references to people and landmarks in the surrounding district, you will find that many folk who would never bother with poetry will be intrigued and buy this. I've worked in several bookshops and seen this happening over and over again.

The advantage with this type of publication is that you can invest all your energy in targeting a relatively small part of the country. You can try to persuade all sorts of different outlets to stock your book; for example if you have three or four poems about the Black Bull pub then get the Black Bull to put a few copies in their window. Local authors are often viewed as celebrities; don't let any opportunity to play on that go by.

A Perthshire author self-published a work on one of the local glens a year or so back. He invested in a quality cover and the book appeared both in hardback and paperback. He did readings for outdoor groups, schools, libraries and churches and after the book had been in print for a year it had sold over two thousand copies. That may not sound like many books, but remember that many mainstream publishers will be satisfied if a first time novelist sells half that number of copies - across the whole of Britain! A local audience is the key to a self-publishing author's success or downfall - bear that in mind at all times.

# Vanity publishing

## MIRANDA PUBLISHING
### NEW YORK - LONDON - SYDNEY

Seeks manuscripts of all types for publications. Memoirs and poetry particularly valued. Growing publisher with world-wide links. No material not considered.

When you see adverts like this, learn to shudder. If you are tempted to respond, then like Odysseus before the Sirens, tie yourself to the mast and refuse to listen. Vanity publishing will only break your heart - and your bank balance.

All sorts of newspapers and literary journals (sadly) carry adverts akin to the fictional one above. No matter how convincing the wording may be, don't believe the blarney.

A vanity publisher may well demand up to several thousand pounds to produce your book. But no matter what may be promised about marketing and distribution, none of it will happen. Nor will the promised agents get your book into the high street shops, for the simple reason that bookshops can smell vanity publishers a mile away, and very rightly want nothing to do with them.

Vanity publications don't know their art from their elbows. They couldn't care less about the quality of the material they receive, only about the quantity of cheques they manage to get hold of. They may give you a list of the people who started off their writing careers by paying to get their first book published, but these are individuals who succeeded despite the vanity publishers, not because of them.

If you are in doubt as to whether or not the operator is a vanity publisher, remember that no mainstream house ever needs to ask for manuscripts - they arrive of their own accord by the sackful. Nor does any editor in his right mind particularly request poetry and memoirs because he would be able to fill the Albert Hall with them after a week. Vanity publishers mention these two genres very cynically in their adverts because they know all too well how difficult the mainstream market is for both poetry and memoirs, and their gleeful hope is that many disillusioned writers will fall into their clutches. And they do, year after year...

I understand how tempting it can be. For several years I was simply desperate to see a first poetry collection in print and I was enraged and grief-stricken every time that precious package of poems came back through the letter-box. I often saw adverts for vanity publishers and the temptation was huge to call a halt to this dreadful waiting and invest my savings in a secret deal. I'm mightily glad that I didn't.

A vanity publication may well come back to haunt you, become a Banquo's ghost you can't get rid of. If the next book you get published is by a mainstream outlet, all sorts of embarrassing and awkward questions may be asked by reviewers and newspaper editors about 'your first book.' Is it worth shelling out three or four figures for a publication which will sell perhaps fifty or a hundred copies? If you believe your work is good, that you have something to say, and that others believe that too, then don't sign in blood the vanity publisher's contract. Keep on fighting to find a reputable outlet, no matter how small it may be, because at the end of the day you will always know your poetry was published because of its merit, not because of your ability to pay.

# The small presses

Another possible publication opportunity lies with the small publishers. There are literally hundreds of such outlets across Britain, often run by individuals already producing small magazines. These are the dedicated soldiers of the poetry world, who work away in lonely, damp attics producing a print-run of a collection of some up-and-coming poet's work.

In many ways it will be easier to have a collection accepted by such an outlet, especially if your work is already known to the editor or has appeared in their magazine. There's no reason why a collection produced in this way shouldn't sell a few hundred copies over time, depending of course on how many readings you can undertake and how much work you can do to publicise the book.

Bear in mind that very few collections of this type will ever end up in shops, except local ones that may be particularly keen to support your writing. I find it very hard to envisage one of the high street chains - even a local branch - taking on a small press publication. Productions will be rarely of a high enough standard to entice them.

Most of the truly small presses will not possess the necessary finance to justify expenditure on marketing and distribution. It will almost certainly be up to you to persuade local libraries and shops to invest in a few copies. I've had to do it myself; apologetically creep into managers' offices, cap in hand, while they moodily scour the pages of my precious work. In time you learn to be bolder, to give as good as you often get.

The terms a small press offers may also be pretty depressing, another reason for negative reactions from the likes of Dillons and Waterstones. The high street bookshops often expect 50% of the retail price, something which even mainstream publishers of poetry books find hard to swallow. Such terms would be impossible for the average small publisher, struggling to recoup production and limited distribution costs.

It's very likely, too, that a small press publisher will not offer royalties; indeed there will be no formal contract to start with. It might well be that in the wake of publication you receive twenty or thirty copies of the print-run in lieu of royalties, and that subsidiary copies will be available to you at a reasonable, discounted price.

All this may sound bleak, but it is the hard reality of small press publishing for both poet and producer. Small press publication does, however, remain an invaluable stepping stone for a new writer onto the first rung of the ladder - a move up towards that moment when a mainstream house finally finds the courage to say yes to your collection. A list of some small publishers appears at the back of this book.

# 6 MARKETING YOURSELF ?

- Signings
- Local radio
- Local papers
- Reviews
- Readings
- Workshops

However you get that first collection published, you must be prepared to push and push again at that huge wooden door which stands in front of most new writers. I know a number of poets who have given up disillusioned, having felt in the end the effort required to succeed was just too much. I suppose it is to some extent a question of an individual's reservoir of self-determination and tenacity how they respond to bad reviews and poor sales. I'm not about to throw any stones at writers for giving up in despair, but it is sad to see talented authors throwing away their swords just when it looked as though the battle was turning in their favour.

One useful trick is to keep a folder of praise mail, something I've done since I started out. Put into this the positive letters from publishers, the personal letters of praise you've received from audience members at readings, or from friends who have truly felt inspired by your writing. When the dragons of despair start to burn away your self confidence, reach for this praise mail and read it until you can get up again onto your literary feet to fight another day.

# Signings

Recently I was asked to do a book signing in one of the main high street bookshops in my local town. It was a week before Christmas and the streets were full to capacity with everyone from the tots to the totterers buying gifts for their nearest and dearest. I reckoned on a fairly good avalanche of books; after all, this was my home territory and the world and his donkey was in town.

I didn't sell one book, not a solitary copy. Mind you, neither did Edwina Currie, I'm glad to say, when she came to do a signing in Edinburgh recently, and I'm sure the bookshop concerned did an awful lot more in the way of advertising beforehand.

I think book signings are best kept local. If you are sitting behind sixty copies of your collection in Waterstones you will almost certainly intimidate people. They will be reluctant to pick up a copy of the book from the table because they feel they will be duty-bound to buy it. Local people will know you, and probably like you, even if they don't particularly like poetry or know your work. You will be something of a rare species among them, and though they may gently mock you to your face, they will probably praise you behind your back. So sign locally, until genuine fame gives you sufficient confidence to take on the towns.

Advertise beforehand, advertise for all you are worth. Get an interview onto local radio, put a piece into your community magazine, and do your own posters if the shop or library giving you the signing will not do so themselves. Best of all, tell people the event is taking place. Jungle drums are still the most effective means of communicating in a local community, whether that community be Kentish Town or Carluke.

Make every effort to be friendly to your customers, not just because it is good to be so, but because they may ask you to do a reading in their town hall at Easter or consider talking to the Women's Guild in November. It's all about little acorns making oak trees, and very few contacts or offers should be considered beneath your dignity.

# Local radio

I've already mentioned this as an important outlet for writers fighting for a platform and for publicity. I used to think that five men and a sheepdog listened to my local radio station, but I've often been suitably chastened after walking down the high street on the morning following an interview to be told by several passers-by that they'd heard me the night before.

More people listen than you imagine. Your book sales will not go up by hundreds, but recognition of your work certainly will.

Of course the first time you go into the studio is nerve-racking. It pays to do a bit of homework beforehand; check with the interviewer, if you can, what sort of framework the interview will have. There's no need to prepare a set of written answers to the questions that may come your way, but it will most likely put you at your ease if you have spent a little time thinking about what you want to say in advance. Be sure to tell the interviewer the sort of questions you would like to be 'fed' beforehand if that is particularly important, especially if you are in the studio to advertise a reading, a signing, or the publication of a book. If this is the case, it is no bad thing to write down the relevant details on a piece of paper so the interviewer can make mention of them accurately on air. If I had a fiver for every time the person concerned tried to quote the details from memory and got them wrong...

Try to get the chance to read from your own work on radio. It's good practice and poems read aloud often have a power of their own. My own feeling is that a particularly evocative and lyrical poem published in a book is not unlike a butterfly pinned to a board: it requires the poet's voice to release it and breathe life back into its wings.

If you simply cannot bring yourself to conquer the fear of doing a broadcast, or if you have tried and the result was too horrible to remember, then do not despair. But do contact them when you have information regarding your readings or signings or successes; the station will have a news desk and you never know how many people may hear and take note.

# Local papers

When considering truly local advertising for your writing, never forget all the newsletters and local rags - which will reach a surprising number of people before they end up in the recycling bin. Just that one weekly paper which lies on the table in the doctor's surgery may be scanned by a hundred or more people.

Make a list of these outlets and find out the names of editors or staff wherever possible. Then call them up, or drop them a line, outlining your success and asking them if they would consider covering the story. There's little point doing all at once; perhaps have a reading written up in one paper, and a visit to a school covered somewhere else.

It's particularly important with papers of any real size and influence to read a copy of what they are planning to say about you before it is published. Journalists have a nasty habit of not being able to read their own shorthand, and I have suffered all too often from book titles being confused, publishers being misspelt, and my own name mangled beyond recognition. It takes just thirty seconds to scan a few paragraphs of prose, and it's worth doing. Cut out and keep pieces that are written about your work, not just for the sake of pride, but because it may prove useful one day. There may come a time when you are asked for quotes about your writing, or when a publisher wants copies of articles from past days.

Again, let these outlets know ahead of time when you are to do a signing or reading locally. Find out the best contacts and make sure they learn your name. Sweeten them up and they can become very useful indeed!

# Reviews

Everyone wants to be reviewed when they first get a book in print, often because they believe sales will be increased dramatically by coverage.

In actual fact I don't believe sales are that affected by reviews, either bad or good. Most published poets I know are fairly nonchalant about the effect of reviews; they usually reckon that word of mouth is a more important factor in selling books by far.

But there's no doubt that it is of importance to be seen to be reviewed. I have waxed lyrical about getting your name known as a poet, and here is a vital area for doing just that.

I remember how frustrated I was after my first poetry collection was published, because I expected the reviews to appear like dew after nightfall and there was nothing. I started off sad, became angry, and eventually began to fight to get editors to take notice of the book.

In my experience, that has always been the best way to ensure that reviews appear. Make a careful list of all the literary outlets, local papers, radio stations and the like which you reckon might have an interest in your book. Try to get your publisher to send off review copies if you can, but face being told to do this yourself if the publisher is small. At any rate, try to get review copies from the publisher free of charge.

Drop each outlet a line introducing yourself and saying a few words about your book, requesting that you would be very grateful if they reviewed your work. Some you will never hear from again, others are almost certain to follow up your approach. In all honesty, the better you have done your homework, the more success you are likely to have.

It goes without saying that you should target the more relevant and significant poetry journals. If your collection comprises nature poems, then *The Countryman* and *This England* should be at the top of your list to receive review copies. If the book is about inner-city deprivation and life on a council estate, then target *Poetry London Newsletter, Iron* and *Stand*. Think hard about where your work is going to be best received. It's better to send out two review copies and get two reviews than to send out twenty and get none.

Is a bad review damaging, or is, as they say, all publicity good publicity? I'm not sure. At the end of the day reviews do not sell books, but they do sell poets. A dreadful review in a prominent journal may wound you and your reputation, but buyers of poetry books will make up their own minds. They may well buy the collection, however bad the reviews, just to see whether those reviews were right or not.

There is no doubt a good review will do you, and your morale, good. To be given recognition, even muted praise, when you are struggling to get a foothold in the poetry world means a great deal indeed. It is formal recognition of you own ability.

So keep these good reviews for the dark days when your poetry thuds down on the mat rejected. They will help convince you it's worth carrying on, that you have what it takes.

# Readings

Once you have a book in print, if not long before, you will be undertaking readings. Try to be as imaginative as possible with these, especially in a local context, because the scope is endless. You will find that women's guilds, retirement groups, youth clubs and church societies can all prove interested audiences. Obviously you must be careful to tailor your reading according to the needs of each group; never become cocky and begin 'recycling' talks. Treat every reading as unique and every person in your audience as an individual; this is no more than you would want or expect if you were one of the audience.

When you have plenty of courage and a good deal of experience, think about undertaking a school reading. Your local authority will be able to give you leads on likely schools, and letters of approach to head teachers are advisable. Bear in mind that after the Dunblane tragedy and other attacks in British classrooms in recent years, staff are extra vigilant about visitors and may want to know more of your background before extending an invitation. My advice is to begin at the top and work your way down. It's easiest to make headway with the oldest pupils, who are likely to be less cynical and more mature. I prefer to speak to a group of youngsters who have opted to come to listen, and not been coerced; a compulsory event will not make your task any the easier.

What do you cover with them? It's simpler for me because I am a writer of novels and children's fiction as well as poetry, but there is plenty of scope for discussion and tuition within poetry alone.

Ask the teacher before you visit the school how you can most assist. Generally I offer to read some pupils' work beforehand, something that is almost always welcomed by the teaching staff and the young writers alike. Think about the story areas of their writing, and start your talk by praising the scope of their imagination, the use of imagery, the bravery of their choice of topics, etc. Then talk about where they might be able to strengthen their poetry, always doing so constructively, without making them feel you have all the answers. Good poetry is in the eye of the beholder; no matter how long our apprenticeship we must not become arrogant as poets.

Try at all times to get them to start talking about and discussing the components of good writing among themselves. (This generally will be made a lot easier if the class teacher is not present to intimidate them, but that is not always possible.) Try to pass on to them something of your enthusiasm for this strange and wonderful poetry-writing life. That is a great privilege.

Conducting readings and workshops in prison is not dissimilar, nor is it much more daunting than facing twenty-five bored teenagers. Going in the gates is of course a trial - if you'll excuse the pun - and the prison environment is challenging to come to terms with. The first time I undertook a workshop in prison I came into the designated room with jelly legs and swam through a blue sea of cigarette smoke to a vacant chair. 'I'm very glad to be here,' I said, making my usual opening remark. 'Well, speak for yourself!' came the quick-witted response from the back.

I think it is even more important in this context that you speak to an audience that has chosen to listen, not been forced at the point of a bayonet. Creative writing is of real importance to prisoners all over the country, and if you visit to offer insight and advice to a writing group you will be given a real welcome. Go into prison as yourself. Don't try to be 'one of them,' having formed a false stereotype beforehand of the 'average prisoner'. You'll find prisoners from every class and every walk of life inside. Be yourself, because they will respect that, whatever your background. I went in trying hard to be long-haired and ordinary; in two minutes they had me sussed out - someone asked which public school I'd been to.

A note on finances: do bear these points in mind when planning readings and workshops for the above groups:

- Visits to schools and prisons generally receive support from the local authority
- Don't be shy to ask about this payment; the labourer is worthy of their hire
- A fee should be payable, in addition to travelling expenses

# Workshops

Workshops for up-and-coming writers can be daunting; I say this from past experience. There is a vast amount of difference between a reading and a workshop. The first you can undertake whenever you feel you have the confidence to share a stage with other poets, or even to go solo. Workshops are much harder work. They require a confidence in your own writing ability and style, a knowledge of how to craft good poetry and hone it effectively, an ability to lead and steer a writing group in a set direction. Given the choice between a reading and a workshop I'd plump for the former every time. But a good workshop can be rewarding and challenging all the same, it depends to a certain extent on the group. It's inadvisable to visit The Feminist Writing Tigresses of Upper Teesdale as a first venture. People are realising more and more the value of poetry and creative writing in general as far as therapy is concerned, and many groups have been started in recent years to encourage those with troubled pasts. The Survivors' Poetry Network, for example, exists to provide both a support and a creative inspiration for people who are survivors, in any sense at all, of mental health problems. Such groups are keen to invite along practising poets to pass on advice and encouragement to members, and often the chance to offer constructive criticism of members' work. Adult education groups are another possible starting point for workshops, or even children's classes if you have experience with that age group from before and have the ability to fire young minds.

Whatever the starting point and however much experience you gain, workshops remain hard work. No two groups are ever the same, so you should never become complacent and begin trying to cut corners by 'recycling' programmes. Prepare as much as you can beforehand, while still being flexible enough to change tack in the course of a workshop if that seems right. Always have more material than you need rather than too little; listen to other leaders of workshops and learn from both what they do well and what they do badly.

Most of all, enjoy every minute of what you do. You are passing on your love of creativity and poetry, and the more you do of that, the more your audience - whoever they are - will respond. Poetry is about life itself - live both to the full!

# 7 A CHECKLIST FOR POETS

- Magazines
- Publishers
- Competitions
- Awards and bursaries
- Other useful organisations
- Foreign journals
- Recommended reading

## Magazines

Horo is a representative selection of well-established poetry magazines:

### Orbis 199
The Long Shoot, Nuneaton, CV11 6JQ.
Quarterly. Very open to poetry by new writers. Includes the work of a feature poet in each issue. *Orbis* is very well-known; be patient when waiting for news of your submission. Small payment made for published poems.

### Iron 5
Marden Terrace, Cullercoats, North Shields, NE30 4PD.
Three issues a year. Particularly keen (one feels) on urban writing and poems and stories with a social edge. Very swift in responding to submissions. Do not submit more than five poems in a batch. Small payment made for published poems.

### Staple
Gilderoy East, Upperwood Road, Matlock, Bath, DE54 3PD.
Three issues a year. Supports both established and up-and-coming poets. Short poems are most likely to succeed here, since space is always at a

premium. Allow up to two months for a response. Small payment made for published poems.

### New Welsh Review

Chapter Arts Centre, Market Road, Cardiff, CF5 1QE. Quarterly. Focuses on Welsh writing but outsiders are definitely welcome. Poems. short stories, articles, interviews and reviews. Waiting for a response can be trying, but do not give up hope. Fairly generous payment made for published poems.

### Chapman 4

Broughton Place, Edinburgh, EH1 3RX. Quarterly. Focuses on Scottish writing but many issues are concerned with wider themes: women's poetry, minority writing, etc. Poems, short stories, articles and reviews. Do not hold your breath waiting for news of a submission; go off and write a novel first. Payment made for published poems.

### Acumen 6

The Mount, Higher Furzeham, Brixham, South Devon, TQ5 8QY. Three issues a year. A very beautiful journal, as likely to accept the work of an unknown as that of the Poet Laureate. Short poems will always succeed best here because of the pressure on space. Always responds to submissions quickly and individually. Small payment, if any, for published poems.

### Envoi

44 Rudyard Road, Biddulph Moor, Stoke-on-Trent, ST8 7JN. Three issues a year. Contains the poetry of both the famous and the new. No particular style favoured, but it would seem gentler and more traditional writing is better liked than the in-your-face poetry of the ultra brash. The editor likes to print a number of poems from each author so work hard to make a submission count. No payment for published poems.

### The Countryman

Sheep Street, Burford, Oxon, OX18 4LH. Six issues a year. Poems are used as 'fillers' here, to follow articles and to enhance photography. All the poems used have an outdoor theme, from harvesting to hearing the first cuckoo of spring. A natural outlet for poets concentrating on rural topics. Payment made for published poems.

### The Haiku Quarterly

39 Exmouth Street, Kingshill, Swindon, SN1 3PU
Quarterly, logically enough! Haiku, Tanka and other minimalist poems. Open to beginners and to Byrons. It can take an awfully long time to hear about a submission, so the impatient are not advised to send work. Token payment is made for published work.

### The Month

114 Mount Street, London, W1Y 6AH
Monthly, of course. Catholic journal edited by the Jesuit Fathers. Articles and poems explore the nature of faith, today's society and cultural development. Always open to sincere thought. Despite a large mailbag, the response time is very good. No payment made for published poems.

If you want a comprehensive list of current poetry magazines, *The Writer's Handbook* is probably best. A useful checklist is also produced by The Poetry Library in London, who provide information too on poetry competitions, festivals, etc. Send a large s.a.e. to: The Poetry Library, Royal Festival Hall, South Bank Centre, London, SE1 8XX.

## Publishers

For mainstream publishers of poetry, I think the best information is to be had from the Writers' and Artists' Yearbook. A regularly updated list is also available from The Poetry Library in London. If you want to see, and browse through, the productions of the leading publishers, then spend a morning in Waterstones or find a specialist poetry bookshop.

For small press publishers turn to *The Writer's Handbook*. Here you will find enough to keep you happy for many moons; the only problem is it is virtually impossible to see the wood for the trees.

The following list comprises reputable, middle-sized presses which may provide that vital stepping stone to a contract with a mainstream publisher.

### The National Poetry Foundation
Johnathon Clifford, 27 Mill Road, Fareham, Hants. PO16 0TH.

### Flambard Press
Peter Lewis, 4 Mitchell Avenue, Jesmond, Newcastle Upon Tyne, NE1 3LA.

### Headland Publications
Gladys Mary Coles, Ty Coch, Galltegfa, Ruthin, Clwyd, LL15 2AR.

### Peterloo Poets
Harry Chambers, 2 Kelly Gardens, Calstock, Cornwall, PL18 9SA.

### Stride Publications
Rupert Loydell, 11 Sylvan Road, Exeter, Devon, EX4 6EW.

### Hippopotamus Press
Roland John, 212 Whitewell Road, Frome, Somerset, BA11 4EL.

### Oasis Books
Ian Robinson, 12 Stevenage Road, London, SW6 6ES.

### The Frogmore Press
Jeremy Page, 42 Morehall Avenue, Folkestone, Kent, CT19 4EF.

### The Women's Press
34 Great Sutton Street, London, EC1V ODX.

### Scottish Cultural Press
Jill Dick, Unit 14, Leith Walk Business Centre, 130 Leith Walk, Edinburgh, EH3 5DT.

# Competitions

The following are but a few of the dozens of poetry competitions run every year in Britain. You will be able to build up a comprehensive list by studying the handbooks and contacting The Poetry Library. Contact individual competitions for entry forms.

### Rhyme International
(For the encouragement of rhyming poetry in general and specialist forms like the sonnet and villanelle.) c/o Orbis, 199 The Long Shoot, Nuneaton, Warwickshire, CV11 6JQ.

**Outposts Competition**
c/o Outposts, 22 Whitewell Road, Frome, Somerset, BA11 4EL.

**The Frogmore Poetry Prize**
The Frogmore Press, 42 Morehall Avenue, Folkestone, Kent, CT19 4EF.

**The National Poetry Competition**
The Poetry Society, 22 Betterton Street, London, WC2H 9BU.

**Staple Open Poetry Competition**
Tor Cottage, 81 Cavendish Road, Matlock, Derbyshire, DE4 3HD.

# Awards and bursaries

**E.C. Gregory**
The most recognised award for younger poets in Britain; five or six poets are chosen each year. Candidates must be British and under the age of thirty at 31 March in the year the Award is made. A collection of not more than thirty poems

must be submitted no later than 31st October to the Society of Authors, 84 Drayton Gardens, London, SW10 9SB.

**The Forward Prizes for Poetry**
These comprise three awards for the best collection of poetry of the year, the best first collection, and the best poem published (but not as part of a collection).
Book Trust, Book House, 45 East Hill, London, SW18 2QZ.

**Arts Council of England**
Awards are made each year to already published writers of poetry, fiction, autobiography or biography. For full details of application procedures contact the Literature Department, Arts Council of England, 14 Great Porter Street, London, SW1P 3NQ.

**Arts Council of Wales Bursaries**
Similar awards are made to writers resident in Wales each year. For further details contact the Arts Council of Wales, Museum Place, Cardiff, CF1 3NX.

## Scottish Arts Council Bursaries

A number of bursaries are awarded to Scottish writers each year. Full details are available from the Scottish Arts Council, Literature Department, 12 Manor Place, Edinburgh, EC3 7DD.

# Other useful organisations

### The Scottish Poetry Library

Tweed Dale Court, 14 High Street, Edinburgh, EH1 1TE.

### Northern Poetry Library

Country Library, The Willows, Morpeth, Northumberland, NE61 1TA.

### The Arvon Foundation

(for all types of residential writing courses)
Totleigh Barton, Sheepwash, Beaworthy, Devon, EX21 5NS.

### Ty Newydd Courses

(similar to Arvon)
Llanystumdwy, Criccieth, Gwynedd, LL52 0LW.

# Foreign journals

As I have already made clear in my section on getting poetry published abroad, the market is huge. Detective work to sound out the best outlets is the only solution. Below are some of the journals I have found most helpful and successful; all are in a good state of health and should survive for many years to come.

### Australia

**Imago**
GPO Box 2434, Brisbane 4001 Queensland.
Bi-annually. This A5 glossy paperback is as handsome as a Penguin book. The contents are divided between short stories and poetry, and the last ten or so pages are devoted to reviews of new Australian publications. But the contributors to *Imago* are a truly international bunch, and there is plenty of scope here for British poets. One of Australia's friendliest outlets. Payment is made for all published work.

## Westerly

Department of English, The University of Western Australia, Nedlands, Western Australia 6907.
Bi-annual. This journal has an international reputation and often contains writing by highly respected authors, Australian and non-Australian alike. It has perhaps more of an academic edge than *Imago*, but high quality poems and short stories will always succeed nonetheless. Payment is made for all published work.

## Northern Perspective

Northern Territory University, PO Box 40146, Casuarina, NT 0811.
Bi-annual. This handsome A4 journal is produced by the Northern Territory University. A great deal of the magazine comprises articles concerned with life in this region of Australia: culture, history, government, etc. But a surprising amount is devoted to poetry, and a good number of foreign poets' work at that. No particular style prevails. Payment is made for all published work.

## Poetry Australia

South Head Press, The Market Place, Berrima, NSW 2577.
Quarterly. This long-established journal publishes both Australian and foreign poetry, and has earned a good reputation over the years for what it chooses to publish. The editor is himself a poet of some standing and has a lot of respect for, and knowledge of, contemporary British poetry. No payment is made for published work.

## Canada

## Queen's Quarterly

Queen's University, Kingston, Ontario, K71.
Has to be Canada's finest literary journal. An A5 production, it contains over 200 pages of articles, interviews, photography and poetry. It has to be said that the poems are rather shoved to the back, and usually number about four or five, but this is a journal well worth trying to get into nonetheless. The editors reply to submissions very quickly, but often poetry is returned simply because they have so much material on their hands.

Payment for published poems is very high.

### The New Quarterly

C/O Elp, Pas 2082, University of Waterloo, Waterloo, Ontario, N21.

Not as glossy as *Queen's*, but a handsome A5 production all the same. There is a far greater accent here on poetry; about half the journal is devoted to this genre, with the rest comprising interviews and a few short stories. Most of the contributors are Canadian, but the editors are very open to submissions from abroad. Payment is made for published poems.

### Green's Magazine

P.O. Box 3236, Regina, Sask. S4P 3HL.

Quarterly. An A5 production which lacks the glamour of either of the first two Canadian journals. It contains a broad mix of short fiction and poetry, from mainly Canadian writers but foreign contributors as well. No payment is made for published work.

## South Africa

### New Coin

ISEA, Rhodes University, PO Box 94, Grahamstown 6140. Appears bi-annually and is produced by Rhodes University Press. The journal is A5 in size and contains somewhat over 100 pages of poetry, short fiction and reviews. By far the greatest percentage of work is by African writers, but the editors are very open to writing from abroad. No payment is made for published work.

# Recommended reading

### Writers' and Artists' Yearbook (Black)

and/or

### The Writer's Handbook (Macmillan).

Try to get hold of the most recent edition possible, since so many poetry outlets and publishers change addresses fairly frequently. Your local library will be able to order copies for you to borrow if they do not already have the books on their shelves.

## *Small Press Guide UK*
(Writers' Bookshop)
This provides much useful information on the small press scene in Britain today; detailed listings of some 500 different literary outlets publishing poetry and short fiction.

## *Small Press Guide US* and *Small Press Guide Australia*
(Writers' Bookshop)
These provide information on hundreds of small magazines in the US and Australia. Invaluable for anyone wanting to try their luck in these poetry markets.

## *Guide to Literary Prizes, Grants and Awards*
(Compiled by Book Trust and the Society of Authors)
This is of particular use when you have a first book in print, to find out the many awards there are for poetry collections on offer.

## *The New Poetry*
(Bloodaxe)
This book provides a useful insight into the work of some of the most noticed poets in Britain today. It has many flaws and many omissions, but it's worth looking at all the same.

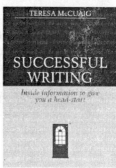